Primarily Problem Solving

Written by
Dianne Draze

Illustrated by
Dean and **Pat Crawford**

ISBN 931724-39-2
© Copyright 1986 Dandy Lion Publications
San Luis Obispo, California

Published by **Dandy Lion Publications**
San Luis Obispo, CA

Table of Contents

For the Instructor

What is Creative Problem Solving?

Creative Problem Solving (CPS) is a process that allows people to apply both creative and rational thinking to find solutions to everyday problems. Creative Problem Solving can eliminate the tendency to approach problems in a haphazard manner and, consequently, prevents surprises and/or disappointment with the solution. It is a way to enhance creative behavior, and it is also a systematic way of organizing information and ideas in order to solve problems. It uses both convergent and divergent thinking. The overall goal of Creative Problem Solving training is to improve creative behavior and problem-solving behavior.

Instructional Objectives

Instructors using *Primarily Problem Solving* to train their students in the Creative Problem Solving process will be providing for the following skills:
1. The ability to read or hear a passage and select relevant information.
2. The ability to summarize information that is presented.
3. The ability to analyze social situations.
4. The ability to think creatively to generate a large number of possibilities (fluency).
5. The ability to think creatively to generate a variety of different possibilities (flexibility).
6. The ability to evaluate options based on given criteria (evaluation).
7. The ability to apply creative thinking to a variety of situations.
8. The ability to plan activities that are relevant to accomplishing a goal.
9. The ability to make inferences.

Creative Problem Solving and the Primary Student

While Creative Problem Solving is a process that is used effectively with adults and is especially useful with businesses, it has applications in the primary classroom. Primary students do face problems and need an effective procedure for dealing with their problems. As a result of training in CPS, primary students are not likely to take out a piece of paper and methodically work through each step of the CPS process every time they sense a problem. They will, however, be able to generalize the procedures of CPS to "think through" a solution rather than indiscriminately latching on to the first or most obvious solution. By introducing CPS to primary students, they will be ready to apply the process to more complicated problems when they reach the intermediate grades. But more important, they will have a sense of control in their lives derived from their ability to deal with difficult situations creatively.

It is advisable to introduce Creative Problem Solving procedures to students in a group lesson, having students pool ideas and recording these ideas on large sheets of paper or an overhead transparency. As students become more familiar with the process, they may work on problems independently, either in small groups or individually. Instructors may, however, wish to make several adjustments to the basic format of this program depending on the skills of students. Some suggested adjustments and applications are:

1. Read the information as a group rather than reading it individually.
2. Go over the information using an overhead projector.
3. Write out the important facts instead of underlining them.
4. Ask for fewer ideas for the "Finding the Problem" and "Finding Ideas" stages.
5. Use group brainstorming for the "Find the Ideas" stage.
6. Provide your own criteria for the "Judging Ideas" stage. Ask students for their ideas for criteria.
7. Have students draw, discuss, or act out instead of writing responses.

8. Use the CPS process on stories used for reading.
9. Use the CPS process to solve classroom problems.
10. Work as a large group.
11. Work in small groups or teams and compare ideas with other groups.

The Creative Problem Solving Process

The Mess

Creative Problem Solving is a five-step process. But before starting with the five steps, students must first select a problem. This is usually called "mess finding." It involves identifying a perplexing situation or a problem that needs solving. Usually people have more problems than they know what to do with, so it is a matter of selecting the most pressing problem. Sometimes, though, people need some help in defining a problem that needs solving. There may be a vague sense of imbalance or uneasiness but the person may not be able to pinpoint the exact nature of the problem. In this situation, it is most helpful to list all the facts and feelings that are associated with the area of concern. In writing "mess" statements, one can either focus on obstacles (things that need to be removed) or outcomes (things you want to attain). In this book, students are given the "mess" statements for the problems. In real life, however, they will be finding their own problems. Their search for problems could be guided by these questions:

- Wouldn't it be nice if...
- I wish I could...
- I don't like it when...
- If I had my way I would...
- The thing that worries me the most is...
- I wish...

- I am unhappy about...
- How can I decide...
- I need to make a change in...
- I am bothered by...
- _____ really bugs me.

Once the problem has been briefly stated using one of these phrases, the student can fill in the facts by answering the questions *who, what, where, when, how,* and *why.*

When the mess has been defined, the student may proceed with the following five steps in the CPS process.

1. Fact Finding

In this step, students find all the important, relevant facts that relate to the problem. If not enough information is provided, students must ask questions that will result in additional information. Students are looking for answers to the questions *who, what where, when, how* and *why.* They make note of factual information, observations, feelings, impressions or inferences, and questions. They look at both what they already know and what they need to find out.

2. Finding the Problem

In this step, students make several problem statements in an attempt to define the "real problem." It is a time to analyze the situation and try to get a better understanding of the entire problem. They look at the problem from several different perspectives and write different "how to" problem statements. The statements should be brief and should lead to many different ideas in the next stage of the process. The most common way to generate problem statements is to complete the statement, "in what ways might I/we..." All statements generated in this step should include ownership (who is involved?) and action (what do they want to do?).

3. Finding Ideas

After selecting the best problem statement, students then think of as many ideas or alternatives as they can to solve the problem. Without analyzing ideas, they try to generate a large number of unusual, unique, creative ideas. They do not think about whether the ideas are good or bad or whether they could work or not. They just try to write down as many ideas as possible. Only after they have created a long list do they select those ideas that seem most workable.

4. Judging Ideas

In this step, students choose the most useful idea. To do this, they first determine appropriate evaluative criteria. Then they use these criteria to systematically rate each idea. Some possibilities for developing criteria are:
- usefulness in accomplishing the objective
- cost in terms of time, money, energy
- necessary materials, equipment, skills
- feelings, values, approval of all people involved
- moral or legal considerations
- timeliness
- consequences (positive or negative)
- how it will affect other people
- difficulty in implementing or feasibility

Once criteria are selected, each idea is rated. For each idea, students ask, "Will the idea...(insert criterion)?" In this way, they determine how well each idea satisfies each criterion. Students then look at the ideas and their ratings and try to find the one best solution—the idea that best meets all the tests or rules. While students are looking for the one best idea, they also need to consider whether two ideas could be combined to make one superior solution or if one idea could be changed in some way to make it the best solution.

5. Plan of Action

In the last step of the process, students outline a plan of action for implementing the idea(s) selected. They consider sources of assistance and potential problems. They make a list of short-term and long-term activities. They also state how they will know if their idea was successful. With this last question, the CPS process becomes a continuing cycle of evaluating where you are and how you can progress to the next level.

Creative Problem Solving		
The Mess select a problem and record information about the problem	**1. Fact Finding** sort out what facts are relevant to the problem and what information is lacking	**2. Finding the Problem** analyze the situation and define the "real problem"
5. Plan of Action plan how to implement the selected solution	**4. Judging Ideas** use criteria to select the best idea	**3. Finding Ideas** think of creative ways to solve the problem

Teaching Notes

The "Mess"

Each problem in this book describes a "mess" situation for students. In addition to the problems that have been presented, students may wish to select personal problems to work on or you may wish to solve a classroom problem using the CPS process. The following is a partial list of potential problems for Creative Problem Solving:

1. Alternate endings for stories from reading lessons
2. Finding new solutions for fables and fairy tales
3. Finding a way to deal with bullying and teasing
4. Completing the sentence, "If I could do anything I would..."
5. Making plans for a club, a hideout, or a party
6. Coming up with ideas for special projects (either for school, scouts, 4-H, holidays, or ways to show someone you care)
7. Finding ways to get what you want—a new bike, a week at camp, a space of your own, an A in spelling...
8. Dealing with common problems like losing classroom balls, failing to return library books on time, keeping a room clean, remembering appointments or assignments, or getting to the bus on time
9. Solving family problems like fighting with siblings, getting chores done, not having a private space, or deciding which TV program to watch
10. Thinking creatively about the statement "I wonder if we/I could..."
11. Completing the sentence, "I wish..."
12. Fulfilling needs like new tennis shoes, more help with math, more freedom to make own decisions, or help with a hobby
13. Overcoming fears and weaknesses
14. Overcoming problems associated with being young, such as being to short, too young, or not skilled enough for some activities
15. Solving logistics problems such as how to get together with friends who live across town or how to reach the top row of elevator buttons
16. Finding creative activities for rainy days, for spring vacation, or for a boring period of time
17. Resolving values conflicts such as what to do when you find a wallet full of money, whether to go to a play with your parents or to a movie with a friend, or whether to spend your allowance on a new toy or buy your sister a birthday present
18. Dealing with situations when things did not go as you planned such as losing your only bus token, forgetting your lunch, getting on the wrong bus, or finding out that the movie you came to see is not playing.

Fact Finding

In most of the problems in this book, students are asked to sort out the relevant information by either underlining the important information or finding the answers to the questions who, what, where, when, how, and why. In addition to finding the important information that relates to each problem, instructors may want to pose some of the following questions or add some of these activities:

1. What are some other things you might need to know before you could solve this problem?
2. Where could you find the answers to these questions?
3. If you were in this situation, how would you feel?
4. Pretend you are in _____'s place and complete this sentence: "I feel...'
5. With a friend, act out a skit that shows the main person discussing the problem with other people (mother, sister, teacher, or an imaginary dog).
6. What other information or feelings might be important?
7. What one fact would you like to add to this problem that could change it in some way?

8. Are there some questions for which you could not find an answer? If so, how could you find the facts you need?
9. What information is the most important (must know) and what information is helpful but not necessary?
10. How would _____ view this problem? With a friend, act out what _____ would say to _____ about this problem.
11. What questions could you ask each character in the story?
12. How would _____'s view of this problem be different than _____'s view? Choose one person and tell how this person would feel.
13. Add two facts or pieces of information that will make this problem one that could happen to you or a friend.
14. What things can you guess about this person or the problem that are not directly stated?
15. If you had to write a newspaper headline for this problem what would it be?
16. Write three more statements that _____ might want to add to the list of facts.
17. What do you know about this problem?
18. What other information do you need? Ask three questions that would provide useful information.
19. Is there anything that you find puzzling about this problem?

Finding the Problem

This step requires students to review the important information they outlined in the last step. Then they must think creatively to pose several possible problem statements. While they are given space to write many statements, they may only write four or five statements. Explain to students that sometimes the problem is not what appears on the surface. Sometimes by stating the problem in several different ways we are able to find a way to look at the problem that will allow us to come up with more ideas than we thought possible. For instance, in the problem with the three little pigs, some possible statements might be:

1. In what ways might the pigs make friends with the wolf?
2. In what ways might the pigs live without going out of the house?
3. In what ways might the pigs outsmart the wolf?
4. In what ways might the pigs get help with their problem?
5. In what ways might the pigs organize the other pigs to help with the problem?
6. In what ways might the pigs encourage the wolf to eat something other than pork?
7. In what ways might the pigs alert the other animals of the danger?
8. In what ways might the pigs alter their lifestyle to deal with the danger?
9. In what ways might the pigs change their home to deal with the danger?
10. In what ways might the pigs reward the wolf for not bothering them?
11. In what ways might the pigs do away with wolves in their town?
12. In what ways might the pigs enjoy a worry-free life?
13. In what ways might the pigs build better homes?

Questions that instructors could use to encourage divergent thinking at this step might include:

1. What is the real problem?
2. Can you state the problem a different way?
3. How else could you view this problem?
4. What are you really trying to do?
5. How would other people view this problem?
6. How could you...? (finish in as many different ways as you can)
7. What do you want to accomplish?
8. Why?

Finding Ideas

At this stage you want to encourage students to think as freely and creatively as possible. Rather than judging ideas, they should try to think of as many unusual ideas as possible. While some ideas may not be usable, they may trigger other ideas that are worthwhile.
    Questions you could use to encourage creative thinking during this stage are:

1. What are all the ideas you can think of?
2. Does that idea make you think of any other ideas?
3. What else comes to mind?
4. What else does that make you think of?
5. How many ways can you complete this sentence: "What if...?"
6. How many ways can you complete this sentence: "Just suppose..."?
7. Can you get any ideas by thinking about something in nature?
8. Can you get any ideas by thinking about _____?
9. What can you use in another way?
10. What can you change in some way?
11. What can be made bigger, stronger, greater, higher, longer, thicker, or more intense?
12. What can be made smaller, lower, weaker, shorter, lighter, or more streamlined?
13. What can you substitute?
14. How can you rearrange things?
15. What could be turned around, upside down, backwards, or inside out?
16. What can you combine?

Judging Ideas

At this point students are attempting to use criteria to select the one best idea. For most of the problems in this book, some criteria have already been given. Students are, however, able to add other criteria that they feel are applicable to the problem. As students become more familiar with the CPS process and begin applying it to their own personal problems, they should begin selecting criteria that are most appropriate to their individual situations. To select criteria, one might consider the following:

1. effects on the objective or goal
2. effects on people
3. effects on costs
4. effects on tangible things—materials, equipment, tools
5. effects on intangible things—opinions, attitudes, values, relationships
6. effects on time

Once students have selected criteria and used them to rate each idea, they will select the idea(s) that they feel best solves the problem. Before selecting the one best idea, you should ask the following:

1. Is there one idea that is the best?
2. Are there two ideas that could be combined to make one great idea?
3. Could you change one idea in some way to make it the best solution?
4. Can you change any of the ideas to make them more usable?
5. Are some of the criteria more important than others? If so, how does that change your selection?

Plan of Action

In writing a plan of action, students must determine what they have to do to put their solution in action. The appropriate questions to ask are:

1. What needs to be done?
2. When does it have to be done?
3. Where do you start?
4. Can you break it down into smaller tasks?
5. What can be done right away?
6. What can be done later?
7. Are there any problems?
8. What could go wrong?
9. Who can help?
10. Who needs to give their approval?
11. Who needs to be "sold" the idea?
12. How will you know if you succeed?
13. Once you've accomplished your goal, what do you do next?

Using Primarily Problem Solving

Flexibility has been designed into Primarily Problem Solving. There are a variety of problems presented and each problem statement is accompanied by worksheets for each step in the CPS process. Instructors who wish to provide guidelines for each step in the process will find all the materials to do this. On the other hand, the format is open enough that at any point instructors may digress from the procedures that have been laid out by substituting a worksheet from the last problem (Your Own Problem). This will allow students more freedom in finding a solution for the problem or by making any other adjustments to accommodate the special needs of students. It is also not necessary to have all students work through each of the problems presented in this book. Instructors may select problems that are most appropriate to students' interests or use some of the problems for a large group presentation of the CPS process, with other problems for individual or small-group exploration.

One set of worksheets has been provided for individual or classroom problems. This set includes the basic format for each step in the CPS process, but teachers and their students have the responsibility to provide the "mess" statement and the criterion as well as ideas that will lead to a satisfactory solution of the problem.

Also included in this book is a section called "Just Problems." This is a set of brief descriptions of problems that could be used in a variety of ways. Some suggestions for use are:

1. Use as "warm ups" for brainstorming, problem finding, or generating questions to provide more information about the problem.
2. Use as additional problems for classroom instruction of the CPS process.
3. Use as discussion starters for sharing feelings, values, and possible solutions.
4. Use as story starters. Ask students to find an acceptable solution to the problem and to write a story about it.
5. Use for "problem of the week." Choose a problem and share it with the class. Also put five large pieces of paper around the classroom. Label each piece to correspond to each step in CPS. As the week progresses, have students add ideas on the pieces of paper. By the end of the week, the group should have a solution for the problem.
6. Use for individual enrichment.
7. Use with the large group for review or to pinpoint where students are having problems with the CPS process.
8. Use as sponge activities to fill spare moments.

Name _____

Jason is 8 years old. His older brother, Brad, is 12 years old. Jason is in the fourth grade. He likes to play baseball and build models. He belongs to Boy Scouts and sings in the church choir. He gets good grades in school. He would like to earn money so he can go to camp this summer. He wants to get a paper route. If he had 30 houses on his route, he could earn $90 per month. Brad has 50 houses on his paper route and makes $150 a month. The newspaper says that you have to be 9 years old to have a paper route. Jason will not be 9 for five more months. Many people tell Jason that he looks older than he really is. He didn't go to camp last year, because he had the measles. He has to have $200 for summer camp in four months. He really wants to go to camp, so he has to find a way to solve his problem.

Underline all the important facts that tell about Jason's problem and that answer these questions—who, what, where, when, why, and how.

   Jason is 8 years old and cannot get a paper route until he is 9. He wants a paper route so he can earn the money he needs to go to camp. Read the important facts about Jason and his paper route problem. Then think about what the "real problem" might be. Write as many ideas as you can by completing this sentence in many different ways:

1. In what ways might Jason _____

2. In what ways might Jason _____

3. In what ways might Jason _____

4. In what ways might Jason _____

5. In what ways might Jason _____

6. In what ways might Jason _____

7. In what ways might Jason _____

8. In what ways might Jason _____

9. In what ways might Jason _____

10. In what ways might Jason _____

Choose the statement that you think best describes the problem.
The "real problem" is _____

_____

Jason's real problem is _____

_____

What are all the ways Jason could solve this problem? What are all the things he could do? Try to think of a lot of creative ideas. Write as many ideas as you can.

1. _____

2. _____

3. _____

4. _____

5. _____

6. _____

7. _____

8. _____

9. _____

10. _____

11. _____

12. _____

13. _____

14. _____

15. _____

If you have more ideas, write them on the back of this sheet of paper.

 Put a * by the ideas you think are the best.

Now that you have made a long list of ideas for Jason, you need to choose the best idea. To do this, you must measure one idea against the others. This is a list of rules or tests that Jason might use to choose the best solution to his problem.

1. The solution gives him the money he needs for camp.

2. The solution should be okay with his parents.

3. The solution should take no more than one hour per day.

4. The solution should not cost any money.

5. The solution should be honest.

Now list your best ideas and rate how each one meets the tests. Use this way of rating the ideas:

+ = very good   0 = okay   − = not very good

Ideas	$200	parents	1 hour	cost	honest

Look at each idea and its ratings. Choose the best idea.
My choice for the best solution is _____

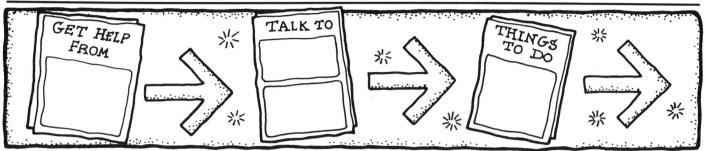

Now it is time for Jason to put his plan into action.
Help him get started by listing the things he has to do.

Plan of Action

Get help from _____

_____

_____

Talk to _____

_____

_____

Things to do now _____

_____

_____

_____

Things to do later _____

_____

_____

_____

Things that might go wrong _____

_____

_____

How Jason will know if his plan is successful _____

_____

Name _____

   Hilary really loves animals—all kinds of animals. At school she
always likes to be the person who takes care of the classroom pets.
She has cared for a bird, gerbils, fish, chicks, a frog, and even a large
black spider. Hilary's birthday is in one month. She is planning a party
at the zoo. Last year she had her party at the skating rink. What
Hilary wants most for her birthday is a pet. She would like to have a
dog or cat. She lives in an apartment, and the owner says, "No pets!"
The apartment owner has a parrot that makes a lot of noise. Another
problem is that Hilary's older sister, Robin, sneezes every time she is
around cats or dogs. Hilary thinks that it is very unfair. She promises
that she will take very good care of the pet.

Underline the most important facts that tell about Hilary's problem
and that answer the questions—who, what, where, when, why,
and how.

Hilary would love to get a pet for her birthday. She lives in an apartment that does not allow pets. Her sister sneezes every time she is around cats or dogs. Read all the important facts about Hilary and her pet problem. Then think about what the "real problem" might be. Write as many ideas as you can by completing this sentence in many different ways:

1. In what ways might Hilary _____

2. In what ways might Hilary _____

3. In what ways might Hilary _____

4. In what ways might Hilary _____

5. In what ways might Hilary _____

6. In what ways might Hilary _____

7. In what ways might Hilary _____

8. In what ways might Hilary _____

9. In what ways might Hilary _____

10. In what ways might Hilary _____

Choose the statement that you think best describes the problem. The "real problem" is _____

_____

19

Hilary's real problem is _____

_____

What are all the things Hilary could do to solve her problem? Think of a lot of creative ideas. Write as many ideas as you can.

1. _____
2. _____
3. _____
4. _____
5. _____
6. _____
7. _____
8. _____
9. _____
10. _____
11. _____
12. _____
13. _____
14. _____
15. _____

If you have more ideas, write them on the back of this sheet of paper.

 Put a * by the ideas you think are the best.

Now that you have made a long list of ideas for Hilary, you need to choose the best idea. To do this, you must measure one idea against the others. This is a list of rules or tests that Hilary might use to select the best solution to her problem.

1. The solution should not make her sister sneeze.

2. The apartment owner should like the solution.

3. The solution should give her a chance to take care of a pet every day.

4. The solution should not cost her parents more than $50.

Now list your best ideas and rate how each one meets the tests. Use this way of rating the ideas:

+ = very good   0 = okay   − = not very good

Ideas	sister	owner	pet	$50

Look at each idea and its rating. Choose the idea that you think is the best.

My choice for the best solution is _____

Now it is time for Hilary to put her plan into action.
Help her get started by listing the things she has to do.

Plan of Action

Get help from _____

_____

_____

Talk to _____

_____

_____

Things to do now _____

_____

_____

_____

Things to do later _____

_____

_____

_____

Things that might go wrong _____

_____

_____

How Hilary will know if her plan is successful _____

_____

Name _____

Sarah is one of the best basketball players in her school. She is tall and usually makes a lot of points for her team. All of her friends tell her how good she is. Sarah would like to try out for the basketball team. The practices for the team are after school on Mondays and Wednesdays from 3:30 p.m. to 4:30 p.m. Sarah takes piano lessons every Monday at 4:00 p.m. She does not like piano, but her mother says that she has to take lessons. She cannot quit. There are basketball teams at other schools that meet on Tuesday and Thursday. Sarah could join these teams, but she could not play with her friends. The games are played on Saturdays. Sarah feels very frustrated. She thinks it would be fun to play on a team with her friends. Also, if she doesn't play on a team this year, she won't gain the skills she needs to play on a team next year. Sarah's brother has played on the basketball team for three years. He does not have to take piano lessons. He plays trumpet with the school band. Sarah and her brother play basketball together.

Underline the most important facts that tell about Sarah's problem and that answer these questions—who, what, where, when, why, and how.

Sarah wants to turn out for the basketball team that practices twice a week after school. One of the practices is at the same time as her piano lesson. Read the important facts about Sarah and her basketball problem. Then think about what the "real problem" might be. Write as many ideas as you can by completing this sentence in many different ways.

1. In what ways might Sarah _____

2. In what ways might Sarah _____

3. In what ways might Sarah _____

4. In what ways might Sarah _____

5. In what ways might Sarah _____

6. In what ways might Sarah _____

7. In what ways might Sarah _____

8. In what ways might Sarah _____

9. In what ways might Sarah _____

10. In what ways might Sarah _____

Choose the statement that you think best describes the problem.
The "real problem" is _____

_____

Sarah's real problem is _____

_____

What are all the things Sarah could do to solve this problem? Think of a lot of creative ideas. Write as many ideas as you can.

1. _____
2. _____
3. _____
4. _____
5. _____
6. _____
7. _____
8. _____
9. _____
10. _____
11. _____
12. _____
13. _____
14. _____
15. _____

If you have more ideas, write them on the back of this sheet of paper.

 Put a * by the ideas you think are the best.

Now that you have made a long list of ideas for Sarah, you need to choose the best idea. To do this, you must measure one idea against the others. This is a list of rules or tests that Sarah might use to select the best solution to her problem.

1. The solution should let her practice her basketball skills.

2. She cannot give up piano lessons.

3. The solution should allow Sarah to play with her friends.

4. She cannot spend more than six hours a week on basketball.

5. _____
    (add your own idea)

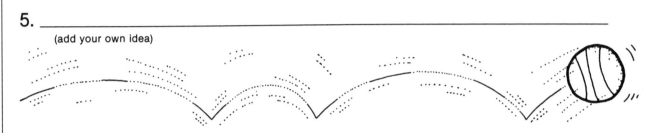

List your best ideas and rate how each one meets the tests. Use this way of rating the ideas:

+ = very good   0 = okay   – = not very good

Ideas	skills	piano	friends	six hours	

Look at each idea and its rating. Choose the best idea.
My choice for the best solution is _____

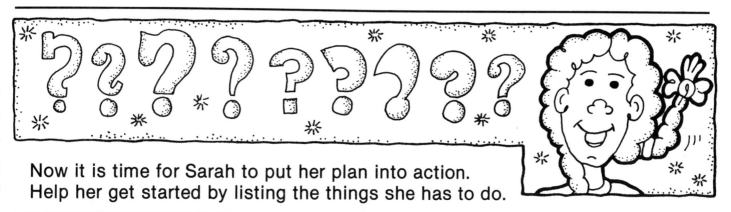

Now it is time for Sarah to put her plan into action.
Help her get started by listing the things she has to do.

Plan of Action

Get help from _____

_____

_____

Talk to _____

_____

_____

Things to do now _____

_____

_____

_____

Things to do later _____

_____

_____

_____

Things that might go wrong _____

_____

_____

How will Sarah know if her plan is successful? _____

_____

Name _____

Ryan is in third grade. His teacher is Miss Turner. He really likes his teacher. He thinks that this is his best year in school. Ryan's mother and father have to leave early for work. He has to wake up and get ready for school by himself. He often oversleeps. Then he is late for school. Miss Turner has told him that if he is late again, he will have to stay after school. If he stays after school, he will be late for baseball practice. If he is late for baseball practice, he will not be able to be on the starting lineup for the game on Saturday. Ryan is embarrassed every time he comes into the classroom late. He does not like Miss Turner to be mad at him. He often stays up until 10:00 p.m. Sometimes he reads and sometimes he watches television. He does not have an alarm in his room. It takes Ryan 25 minutes to walk to school. He cannot ride his bike to school until he is in fourth grade.

Underline the most important facts that tell about Ryan's problem and that answer these questions—who, what, where, when, why, and how.

Ryan often oversleeps in the morning and is late for school. If he is late one more time, he will have to stay after school. Read the important facts about Ryan and his tardiness problem. Then think about what the "real problem" might be. List as many ideas as you can by completing this sentence in many different ways.

1. In what ways might Ryan _____

2. In what ways might Ryan _____

3. In what ways might Ryan _____

4. In what ways might Ryan _____

5. In what ways might Ryan _____

6. In what ways might Ryan _____

7. In what ways might Ryan _____

8. In what ways might Ryan _____

9. In what ways might Ryan _____

10. In what ways might Ryan _____

Choose the statement that you think best describes the problem.
The real problem is_____

_____

Ryan's real problem is _____

What are all the things Ryan could do to solve his problem? Try to think of a lot of creative ideas. Write as many ideas as you can.

1. _____
2. _____
3. _____
4. _____
5. _____
6. _____
7. _____
8. _____
9. _____
10. _____
11. _____
12. _____
13. _____
14. _____
15. _____

If you have more ideas, write them on the back of this sheet of paper.

 Put a * by the ideas you think are the best.

Now that you have made a long list of ideas for Ryan, you need to choose the best idea. To do this, you must measure one idea against the others. This is a list of rules or tests that Ryan might use to select the best solution to his problem.

1. He needs to get to school on time.

2. He needs to go to baseball practice.

3. He cannot make his parents late for work.

4. The solution should be something he can start right away.

5. _____
   (add your own idea)

List your best ideas and rate how each one meets the tests. Use this way of rating the ideas:

+ = very good   0 = okay   − = not very good

Ideas	on time	practice	parents	now	

Look at each idea and its rating. Choose the idea that you think is the best.

My choice for the best solution is _____

Now it is time for Ryan to put his plan into action.
Help him get started by listing the things he has to do.

Plan of Action

Get help from _____

_____

_____

Talk to _____

_____

_____

Things to do now _____

_____

_____

_____

Things to do later _____

_____

_____

_____

Things that might go wrong _____

_____

_____

How Ryan will know if his plan is successful _____

_____

Name _____

Once upon a time there was a beautiful young girl who lived with her mean stepmother and two ugly step sisters. They made her do all the work around the house. Because she was often covered with dirt and soot, they called her Cinderella. One day they received an invitation to a special party at the castle. The prince invited all young girls in the country to his ball. The two ugly sisters were very excited. They made Cinderella work very hard to get them ready to go to the ball. In fact, she was so busy getting them ready that she did not have time to get ready herself. When it was time to leave for the ball, Cinderella was still in rags. She was very sad and disappointed as she waved goodbye to her sisters. They were glad that she was not going with them. They were very jealous of her beauty and good nature. Since she did not have a nice dress to wear to the ball, Cinderella thought it was hopeless to even think about going. The ball was starting in half an hour, and she could never get ready in time.

Underline all of the most important facts that tell about Cinderella's problem and that answer the questions—who, what, where, when, why, and how.

Cinderella would like to go to the party and meet the prince. Her sisters do not want her to go to the party. It's time for the party and Cinderella does not have a dress to wear. Read all the important facts about Cinderella and her party problem. Then think about what the "real problem" might be. Write as many ideas as you can by finishing this sentence in many different ways.

1. In what ways might Cinderella _____

2. In what ways might Cinderella _____

3. In what ways might Cinderella _____

4. In what ways might Cinderella _____

5. In what ways might Cinderella _____

6. In what ways might Cinderella _____

7. In what ways might Cinderella _____

8. In what ways might Cinderella _____

9. In what ways might Cinderella _____

10. In what ways might Cinderella _____

Choose the statement that you think best describes the problem.
The "real problem" is _____

_____

Cinderella's real problem is _____

_____

What are all the things Cinderella could do to solve this problem?
Think of a lot of creative ideas. Write as many ideas as you can.

1. _____

2. _____

3. _____

4. _____

5. _____

6. _____

7. _____

8. _____

9. _____

10. _____

11. _____

12. _____

13. _____

14. _____

15. _____

If you have more ideas, write them on the back of this sheet of paper.

 Put a * by the ideas you think are the best.

Now that you have made a long list of ideas for Cinderella, you need to choose the best idea. To do this, you must measure one idea against the others. This is a list of rules or tests that Cinderella might use to select the best solution to her problem.

1. The solution should not depend on magic.
2. The solution should be something she can do in a short amount of time.
3. The solution should not cost any money.
4. The solution should give Cinderella a chance to meet the prince.

5. _____
(add your own idea)

List your best ideas and rate how each one meets the tests. Use this way of rating the ideas:

   + = very good   0 = okay   − = not very good

Ideas	magic	do now	no cost	prince	

Look at each idea and its rating. Choose the idea you think is the best.

My choice for the best solution is _____

Now it is time for Cinderella to put her plan into action.
Help her get started by listing the things she has to do.

Plan of Action

Get help from _____

_____

_____

Talk to _____

_____

_____

Things to do now _____

_____

_____

_____

Things to do later _____

_____

_____

_____

Things that might go wrong _____

_____

_____

How Cinderella will know if her plan is successful _____

_____

Name _____

Once upon a time, long ago, there was a girl named Rapunzel.
Because of a bad deal her father made with a witch, Rapunzel had to
live with the witch. She was very beautiful, and the witch was very
jealous of her. The witch finally decided to lock Rapunzel up so no
one would ever find her. She locked her in a tower that had no door,
no stairway, and only one window. Every day when the witch came,
she would say, "Rapunzel, Rapunzel, let down your hair." Then she
would climb up to the tower window on Rapunzel's long hair.
Rapunzel was very lonely and longed to escape from the tower. She
wanted to talk to other people, to be free to do all the things that
other people did. But no one knew she was in the tower, so there was
little hope that someone would come and save her. She had no
money. She didn't receive any mail. The only things she knew how to
do were read, write, sew and weave. The situation looked very
gloomy. What could she do?

Underline the important facts that tell about Rapunzel's problem and
that answer these questions—who, what, where, when, why, and
how.

Rapunzel is locked in a tower with no way to get out. She is very lonely and wants to meet other people. Read the important facts about Rapunzel and her problem. Then think about what the "real problem" might be. List as many ideas as you can by completing this sentence in many different ways.

1. In what ways might Rapunzel _____

2. In what ways might Rapunzel _____

3. In what ways might Rapunzel _____

4. In what ways might Rapunzel _____

5. In what ways might Rapunzel _____

6. In what ways might Rapunzel _____

7. In what ways might Rapunzel _____

8. In what ways might Rapunzel _____

9. In what Ways might Rapunzel _____

10. In what ways might Rapunzel _____

Choose the statement that you think best describes the problem.
The "real problem" is _____

_____

Rapunzel's real problem is _____

_____

What are all the things Rapunzel could do to solve this problem?
Think of a lot of creative ideas. Write as many ideas as you can.

1. _____
2. _____
3. _____
4. _____
5. _____
6. _____
7. _____
8. _____
9. _____
10. _____
11. _____
12. _____
13. _____
14. _____
15. _____

If you have more ideas, write them on the back of this sheet of paper.

 Put a * by the ideas you think are the best.

Now that you have made a long list of ideas for Rapunzel, you need to choose the best idea. To do this, you must measure one idea against the others. This is a list of rules or tests that Rapunzel might use to select the best solution to her problem.

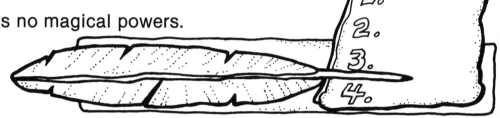

1. The solution cannot cost any money.
2. The witch cannot know what Rapunzel is doing.
3. There should be no danger of Rapunzel getting hurt.
4. The solution has to be done from the tower.
5. Rapunzel has no magical powers.

Now list your best ideas and rate how each one meets the tests. Use this way of rating the ideas:

+ = very good   0 = okay   – = not very good

Ideas	money	witch	danger	tower	magic

Look at each idea and its rating. Choose the idea that you think is the best.

My choice for the best solution is _____

Now it is time for Rapunzel to put her plan into action.
Help her get started by listing the things she has to do.

Plan of Action

Get help from _____

_____

_____

Talk to _____

_____

_____

Things to do now _____

_____

_____

_____

Things to do later _____

_____

_____

_____

Things that might go wrong _____

_____

_____

How Rapunzel will know if her plan is successful _____

_____

          © Copyright 1986 Dandy Lion Publications—**Primarily Problem Solving**

Name _____

    Once upon a time there were three little pigs. When they were old enough, they left their mother's home and went out to make a living for themselves. One little pig made a house that was cheap and easy. It was made out of straw. The second little pig made a house out of wood, because he got a good deal on some used lumber. The third little pig spared no expense and made his house out of bricks. Also living in the neighborhood was a big, bad wolf who was determined to get the three pigs. First he blew down the straw house. Then he blew down the stick house. When both pigs escaped, he went after all three pigs who were now living together in the brick house. He was unable to blow down the brick house. But the pigs knew that they were not safe. They knew that the wolf was a bully and would try to get them every time they left the safe, strong house. The wolf was bigger and faster than the pigs. The pigs, however, were smarter than the wolf and had the law on their side. They knew they had a problem, but they didn't know what to do.

Underline the most important facts that tell about the pigs' problem and that answer these questions—who, what, where, when, why, and how.

The three little pigs got away from the wolf by hiding in the brick house. They know that if they come out, the wolf will try to get them. Read all the important facts about the three little pigs and their problem. Then think about what the "real problem" might be. List as many ideas as you can by finishing the sentence in many different ways.

1. In what ways might the pigs _____

2. In what ways might the pigs _____

3. In what ways might the pigs _____

4. In what ways might the pigs _____

5. In what ways might the pigs _____

6. In what ways might the pigs _____

7. In what ways might the pigs _____

8. In what ways might the pigs _____

9. In what ways might the pigs _____

10. In what ways might the pigs _____

Choose the statement that you think best describes the problem.
The "real problem" is _____

_____

The pigs' real problem is _____

_____

What are all the things the pigs could do to solve their problem?
Think of a lot of creative ideas. Write as many ideas as you can.

1. _____

2. _____

3. _____

4. _____

5. _____

6. _____

7. _____

8. _____

9. _____

10. _____

11. _____

12. _____

13. _____

14. _____

15. _____

If you have more ideas, write them on the back of this sheet of paper.

 Put an * by the ideas you think are the best.

Now that you have made a long list of ideas for the pigs, you need to choose the best idea. To do this, you must measure one idea against the others. This is a list of rules or tests that the pigs might use to select the best solution to their problem.

1. The solution should not cause injury or harm to anyone.

2. The solution should solve the problem for a long time.

3. The solution should not cost more that $50.

4. Mother Pig should approve of the solution.

5. _____
   (add your own idea)

   _____

List your best ideas and rate how each one meets the tests. Use this way of rating the ideas:

+ = very good   0 = okay   – = not very good

Ideas	harmful	time	$50	Mother	

Look at each idea and its ratings. Choose the idea that you think is the best.

My choice for the best solution is _____

_____

Now it is time for the pigs to put their plan into action.
Help them get started by listing the things they have to do.

Plan of Action

Get help from _____

_____

_____

Talk to _____

_____

_____

Things to do now _____

_____

_____

_____

Things to do later _____

_____

_____

_____

Things that might go wrong _____

_____

_____

How the pigs will know if their plan is successful _____

_____

Name _____

Once upon a time, long ago, there was a handsome prince. This prince was always playing tricks on people. Most people didn't mind his tricks. They just laughed when he played tricks on them. One day, though, he played a trick on a cranky old witch. She did not think it was funny. She was so mad at the prince that she cast a spell on him. She turned him into a frog. She said that he must live in the lily pond until a beautiful princess kissed him and broke the spell. So the prince sits on a lily pad each day, wishing that he could return to his life as a prince. He does not like being a frog. He is always cold, he is afraid of deep water, and he hates eating bugs. In the two years since he has been a frog, no beautiful princesses have come to the lily pond. It seems like he is doomed to be a frog forever unless he can think of something to do.

Underline the most important facts that tell about the prince's problem and that answer the questions—who, what, where, when, why, and how.

The young prince has been turned into a frog. He spends his days in the lily pond instead of in the castle. He is very unhappy being a frog. Read all the important facts about the prince and his problem. Think about what the "real problem" might be. List as many ideas as you can by finishing this sentence in many different ways:

1. In what ways might the prince _____

2. In what ways might the prince _____

3. In what ways might the prince _____

4. In what ways might the prince _____

5. In what ways might the prince _____

6. In what ways might the prince _____

7. In what ways might the prince _____

8. In what ways might the prince _____

9. In what ways might the prince _____

10. In what ways might the prince _____

Choose the statement that you think best describes the problem.
The "real problem" is _____

_____

The prince's real problem is _____

_____

What are all the things the prince could do to solve his problem?
Think of a lot of creative ideas. Write as many ideas as you can.

1. _____
2. _____
3. _____
4. _____
5. _____
6. _____
7. _____
8. _____
9. _____
10. _____
11. _____
12. _____
13. _____
14. _____
15. _____

If you have more ideas, write them on the back of this sheet of paper.

 Put a * by the ideas you think are the best.

Now that you have made a long list of ideas for the prince, you need to choose the best idea. To do this, you must measure one idea against the others. This is a list of rules or tests that the prince might use to select the best solution to his problem.

1. The solution should make the prince happy.

2. The solution should not cost any money.

3. The solution should be something a frog can do.

4. _____
   (add your own idea)

5. _____
   (add your own idea)

List your best ideas and rate how each one meets the tests. Use this way of rating the ideas:

　+ = very good　　　　　0 = okay　　　　　− = not very good

Ideas	happy	no cost	can do		

Look at each idea and its ratings. Choose the idea you think is the best.

My choice for the best solution is _____

_____

Now it is time for the prince to put his plan into action. Help him get started by listing the things he has to do.

Plan of Action

Get help from _____

_____

_____

Talk to _____

_____

_____

Things to do now _____

_____

_____

_____

Things to do later _____

_____

_____

_____

Things that might go wrong _____

_____

_____

How the prince will know if his plan is successful _____

_____

Name _____

Here is a list of facts and feelings that Mike has written down about his problem. Read the list.

1. I have to share room with brother.
2. My brother is a pill.
3. My brother rips up my homework.
4. I yell at my brother a lot.
5. Mom is usually busy doing other things.
6. My brother is very fast.
7. My brother thinks it's funny to make me mad.
8. If I don't do my homework I'll get in trouble.
9. I want to get good grades.
10. I wish I had my own room with a lock on the door.
11. My sister has her own room.
12. I'll be 9 in two months.
13. I'd rather watch TV than copy over my homework.
14. I know he does it on purpose.
15. My brother is 1 year old.
16. My brother never bothers my sister's dolls.
17. My sister is 5 years old.

Underline the most information that tells about Mike's problem and that answers these questions—who, what, where, when, why, and how.

   Mike does not like sharing his room with his brother. His brother always rips up his homework. If Mike does not have his homework, he gets in trouble in school. Read all the important facts about Mike and his problem. Then think about what the "real problem" might be. List as many ideas as you can by finishing this sentence in many different ways.

1. In what ways might Mike _____

2. In what ways might Mike _____

3. In what ways might Mike _____

4. In what ways might Mike _____

5. In what ways might Mike _____

6. In what ways might Mike _____

7. In what ways might Mike _____

8. In what ways might Mike _____

9. In what ways might Mike _____

10. In what ways might Mike _____

Choose the statement that you think best describes the problem.

The real problem is _____

_____

Mike's real problem is _____

_____

What are all the things Mike could do to solve his problem? Think of
a lot of creative ideas. Write as many ideas as you can.

1. _____
2. _____
3. _____
4. _____
5. _____
6. _____
7. _____
8. _____
9. _____
10. _____
11. _____
12. _____
13. _____
14. _____
15. _____

If you have more ideas, write them on the back of this sheet of paper.

 Put a * by the ideas you think are the best.

Now that you have made a long list of ideas for Mike, you need to choose the best idea. To do this, you must measure one idea against the others. This is a list of rules or tests that Mike might use to select the best solution to his problem.

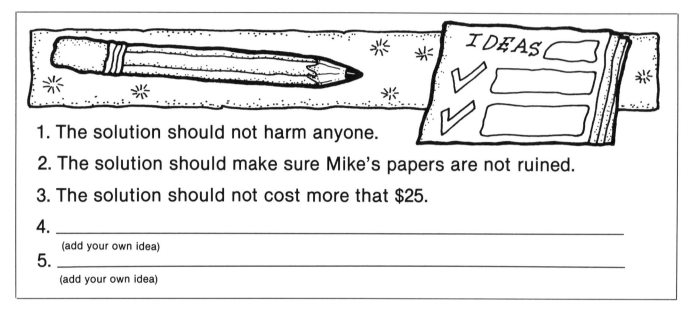

1. The solution should not harm anyone.

2. The solution should make sure Mike's papers are not ruined.

3. The solution should not cost more that $25.

4. _____
   (add your own idea)

5. _____
   (add your own idea)

List your best ideas and rate how each one meets the tests. Use this way of rating the ideas:

+ = very good   0 = okay   − = not very good

Ideas	no harm	papers	$25		

Look at each idea and its ratings. Choose the idea that you think is the best.

My choice for the best solution is _____

_____

Now it is time for Mike to put his plan into action. Help him get started by listing the things he has to do.

Plan of Action

Get help from _____

_____

_____

Talk to _____

_____

_____

Things to do now _____

_____

_____

_____

Things to do later _____

_____

_____

_____

Things that might go wrong _____

_____

_____

How Mike will know if his plan is successful _____

_____

Name _____

Here is a list of facts that tell about a problem. Read the list.

1. My favorite program is "Travels with Charlie."

2. It's about a boy and his dog.

3. It's part comedy and part adventure.

4. It's on Wednesday nights at 7:30 p.m.

5. I am in fourth grade.

6. I have to get ready for bed at 8:00 p.m. each night.

7. I have to do about half an hour of homework each night.

8. We always have a spelling test on Thursdays.

9. I have to study hard for spelling tests.

10. I have to practice piano for half an hour five days a week.

11. My piano lesson is on Monday.

12. I go to soccer practice three times a week for one hour.

13. I get to watch only one hour of television each day.

14. I usually watch television for half an hour when I come home .

15. I would rather do homework than practice piano.

16. Sometimes I have to do the dishes after dinner.

17. I never get to watch my favorite show because I have to do my homework and practice the piano.

Underline the facts about this problem that you think are most important and that answer these questions—who, what, where, when, why, and how.

You like to watch your favorite TV show on Wednesday nights. You don't get to watch the show often because you have to practice piano and do homework. Read the important facts about the problem on Wednesday nights. Then think about what the "real problem" might be. List as many ideas as you can by finishing this sentence in many different ways:

1. In what ways might I _____

2. In what ways might I _____

3. In what ways might I _____

4. In what ways might I _____

5. In what ways might I _____

6. In what ways might I _____

7. In what ways might I _____

8. In what ways might I _____

9. In what ways might I _____

10. In what ways might I _____

Choose the statement that you think best describes the problem.

The "real problem" is _____

_____

Your real problem is _____

_____

What are all the things you could do to solve this problem? Think of
a lot of creative ideas. Write as many ideas as you can.

1. _____

2. _____

3. _____

4. _____

5. _____

6. _____

7. _____

8. _____

9. _____

10. _____

11. _____

12. _____

13. _____

14. _____

15. _____

If you have more ideas, write them on the back of this sheet of paper.

 Put a * by the ideas you think are the best.

Now that you have made a long list of ideas for yourself, you need to choose the best idea. To do this, you must measure one idea against the others. This is a list of rules or tests that you might use to select the best solution to your problem.

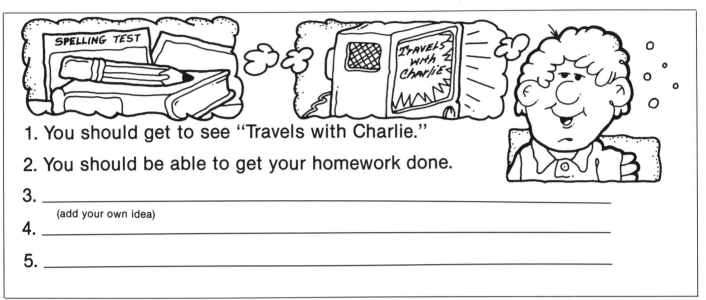

1. You should get to see "Travels with Charlie."

2. You should be able to get your homework done.

3. _____
   (add your own idea)

4. _____

5. _____

List your best ideas and rate how each one meets the tests. Use this way of rating the ideas:

+ = very good   0 = okay   − = not very good

Ideas	TV	work			

Look at each idea and its ratings. Is there one idea that is the best idea?

My choice for the best solution is _____

_____

Now it is time for you to put your plan into action. You can get started by listing the things you have to do.

Plan of Action

Get help from _____

_____

_____

Talk to _____

_____

_____

Things to do now _____

_____

_____

_____

Things to do later _____

_____

_____

_____

Things that might go wrong _____

_____

_____

How you will know if your plan is successful _____

_____

Name _____

Here is a list of thoughts that Bill has written about his problem.
Read the list.

1. Mindy is my older sister. She is 13 years old.

2. Mindy can be really crabby and hard to get along with.

3. I wish I had a brother instead of a sister.

4. Mindy went to camp for two weeks.

5. She promised to bring me a camp sweatshirt if I took care of her plants.

6. The plants died.

7. The plants were a 4-H project.

8. She was going to enter the plants in the fair.

9. The fair is in three weeks.

10. Mindy is going to be mad.

11. I really wanted the sweatshirt.

12. I forgot to water the plants.

13. It has been really hot the past two weeks.

14. I wish I could go to camp.

15. Mom and Dad will take Mindy's side—they always do.

16. I feel badly about killing the plants.

17. My 4-H project is a wooden bird house.

Underline the facts about this problem that you think are the most
important and that answer these questions—who, what, where, when,
why, and how.

Bill agreed to take care of his sister's plants while she was at camp. He forgot to water them, and they all died. She will be coming home soon and will be mad when she finds dead plants. Read all the important information about Bill's problem. Then think about what the "real problem" might be. List as many ideas as you can by finishing this sentence in many different ways:

1. In what ways might Bill _____

2. In what ways might Bill _____

3. In what ways might Bill _____

4. In what ways might Bill _____

5. In what ways might Bill _____

6. In what ways might Bill _____

7. In what ways might Bill _____

8. In what ways might Bill _____

9. In what ways might Bill _____

10. In what ways might Bill _____

Choose the statement that you think best describes the problem.

The "real problem" is _____

_____

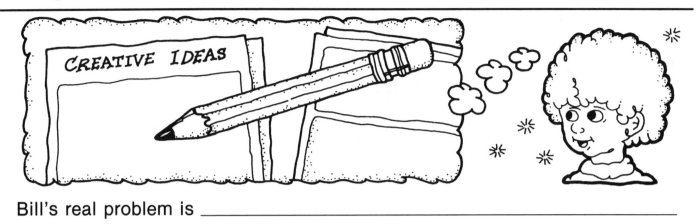

Bill's real problem is _____

_____

What are all the things Bill could do to solve this problem? Think of a lot of creative ideas. Write as many ideas as you can.

1. _____
2. _____
3. _____
4. _____
5. _____
6. _____
7. _____
8. _____
9. _____
10. _____
11. _____
12. _____
13. _____
14. _____
15. _____

If you have more ideas, write them on the back of this sheet of paper.

 Put a * by the ideas you think are the best.

65

Now that you have made a long list of ideas for Bill, you need to choose the best idea. To do this, you must measure one idea against the others. Make a list of four or five rules or tests that Bill might use to select the best solution to his problem.

1. _____

2. _____

3. _____

4. _____

5. _____

List your best ideas and rate how each one meets the tests. Use this way of rating the ideas:

+ = very good   0 = okay   − = not very good

Ideas					

Look at each idea and its ratings. Is there one idea that is the best idea?

My choice for the best solution is _____

Now it is time for Bill to put his plan into action.
Help him get started by listing the things he has to do.

Plan of Action

Get help from _____

_____

_____

Talk to _____

_____

_____

Things to do now _____

_____

_____

_____

Things to do later _____

_____

_____

_____

Things that might go wrong _____

_____

_____

How Bill will know if his plan is successful _____

_____

Name _____

Do you have something that is causing you trouble? Do you have a problem you would like to solve? Write down all your thoughts and feelings and all the facts you can think of that tell about the problem. Try to answer the questions who, what, where, when, why, and how.

_____

_____

_____

_____

_____

_____

_____

_____

_____

_____

_____

_____

Put a * by the information you think is most important.

Let's think more about the problem you are working on. Read all the important facts you listed. Think about what the "real problem" might be. List as many ideas as you can by finishing this sentence in as many different ways as you can:

1. In what ways might I/we _____

2. In what ways might I/we _____

3. In what ways might I/we _____

4. In what ways might I/we _____

5. In what ways might I/we _____

6. In what ways might I/we _____

7. In what ways might I/we _____

8. In what ways might I/we _____

9. In what ways might I/we _____

10. In what ways might I/we _____

Choose the statement that you think best describes the problem.

The "real problem" is _____

_____

Your real problem is _____

_____

What are all the ways you could solve this problem? What are all the
things you could do? Think of a lot of creative ideas. Write as many
ideas as you can.

1. _____

2. _____

3. _____

4. _____

5. _____

6. _____

7. _____

8. _____

9. _____

10. _____

11. _____

12. _____

13. _____

14. _____

15. _____

If you have more ideas, write them on the back of this sheet of paper.

 Put a * by the ideas you think are the best.

Now that you have made a long list of ideas for your problem, you need to choose the best idea. To do this, you must decide on some way to measure one idea against the others. Make a list of four or five rules or tests that you might use to select the best solution.

1. The solution should _____

2. The solution should _____

3. The solution should _____

4. The solution should _____

5. The solution should _____

List your best ideas and rate how each one meets the tests. Use this way of rating the ideas:

+ = very good   0 = okay   − = not very good

Look at each idea and its ratings. Is there one idea that is the best idea?

My choice for the best solution is _____

_____

Name _____

Now it is time for you to put your plan into action.
You can get started by listing the things you have to do.

Plan of Action

Get help from _____

_____

_____

Talk to _____

_____

_____

Things to do now _____

_____

_____

_____

Things to do later _____

_____

_____

_____

Things that might go wrong _____

_____

_____

How you will know if your plan is successful _____

_____

Just Problems 1   **Soccer Team**

You would really like to be on the soccer team. Your friends are on the team and it is a game that you like to play. The problem is that you are not a very good player. You are afraid to try out for the team, because you don't want the other players to make fun of you because you can't play as well as they can. You also don't want to try out for the team if the coach won't let you play in the games.

- -

Just Problems 2   **Pet Snake**

You love snakes. You would love to have a snake for a pet. The only trouble is that your mother is afraid of snakes. She doesn't even like to see pictures of them in books. She says that you cannot have a pet snake. You think that this is very unfair. You have promised that you will keep the snake out of your mother's sight, but she still says, "No snake!"

- -

Just Problems 3   **A New Bike**

You think that you need a new bike. Your old bike is so small that you hit your knees on the handlebars. Your parents say that they cannot afford a new bike now. They want you to wait until your birthday, but your birthday is nine months away. You don't want to ride your old bike for nine more months.

- -

Just Problems 4   **Mean Dog**

You have to walk to school every day. There is a mean dog that lives in one of the houses that you have to pass. Sometimes the dog is locked up. When he is not locked up, he runs out and barks and snarls at you when you walk by. You are afraid that the dog is going to bite you some day. You are very worried about the dog.

Just Problems 5 — Picture Taking

You are very interested in photography. You have read a couple of books about it. You would like to learn how to take pictures. Your sister has a camera, but she won't let you borrow it because you don't know how to use it. She is afraid that you will break it. You know that you could learn how to use a camera if only she would let you use hers. But without a camera you think it would be very hard to learn about taking pictures.

··

Just Problems 6 — Ugly Clothes

Your problem is your clothes. Your mother buys all of your clothes. She usually picks out ugly clothes. At least you think they are ugly. She won't let you pick out the clothes. She says as long as she is paying for them, she gets to choose them. Since you don't have any clothes other than the ones your mother buys, you are stuck wearing clothes that you hate.

··

Just Problems 7 — Haircut

Your problem is your father and his funny ideas about haircuts. Each summer he makes you get your hair cut very, very short. He says that this is the best haircut for summer, when the weather is hot and you spend a lot of time swimming. You have very big ears and you think that this haircut makes you look funny. The other kids always tease you. You are embarrassed and wish you could do something about the situation.

··

Just Problems 8 — Playground Problems

Your class has a problem. They have only one long rope and two balls. Each recess it seems like the same people take the balls and the rope. They let their friends join in the games, but they don't let everyone who wants to play join the games. This leaves a lot of people from your room standing around at recess with nothing to do. It is very boring for these people.

Just Problems 9   Bus Ride

Each day you ride the bus home from school. To take the bus, you must either have a bus token or 50 cents (in exact change). As you get ready to go home, you remember that you forgot to get a bus token this morning. You cannot call your parents to come and pick you up from school because they are at work. You have a dollar bill in your pocket, but the bus driver will not make change. How will you get home?

. . . .

Just Problems 10   Class Play

Your class is making preparations for its annual class play. You would love to have the leading part in the play. You spend a lot of time dreaming about what fun it would be. The problem is that you cannot sing or dance very well and the part requires both singing and dancing. While you want the part, you do not want to make a fool of yourself in front of your classmates and parents.

. . . .

Just Problems 11   No Show

Your mother has just dropped you and a friend off at the theater to see a movie. She will do some shopping while you are in the movie and will be back in two hours. You have just found out that the movie you came to see is not playing. Instead there is an adult movie playing — one that you are not allowed to see. It is very cold and raining very hard, so you don't want to stand around and wait for two hours.

. . . .

Just Problems 12   Art Show

Tomorrow your class is having an art show. It is an important event and prizes are given for the best art projects. You are working on an art project that you think is the best one in the class. You know that it could win a prize and that would make you feel very proud. But because you were absent, you are not finished with your project. There is only 10 minutes left for your art class and you know that you cannot finish in that amount of time.

Just Problems 13   Spiders

You have just moved into a new bedroom that your parents fixed up especially for you in the basement. You are very happy about finally having a room of your own. You discover, however, that there are spiders in your room. You hate spiders! You are dreadfully afraid of spiders! You don't know how you will be able to sleep in a room that has spiders in it. If you complain to your parents, they might give the room to your brother and then you would have to share a room with your baby brother who cries and always messes up your things.

Just Problems 14   Birthday Present

You have been saving for a long time and finally have $5 in your bank account. You have just been invited to a birthday party for your best friend. You want to bring a nice present for this special friend. You also want to buy something for yourself that costs $3. If you buy what you want for yourself, you will not have enough money to buy your friend a nice gift.

Just Problems 15   Computer Class

You are very interested in computers. You have found a computer class for students your age and you want to take the class. Your parents say that you can go to the class. The teacher says that it would be helpful to have a computer at home, so you can practice what you learn in class. Your parents say that you cannot have a computer. You really want to take this class and think that you can do well in it, but you don't know where you can find a computer.